Stark County District Library
www.StarkLibrary.org
330.452.0665

Y0-CJG-661

MAY -- 2019

LET'S FIND OUT! BIOMES

WHAT ARE TEMPERATE DECIDUOUS FORESTS?

HEATHER MOORE NIVER

Britannica
Educational Publishing

IN ASSOCIATION WITH

ROSEN
EDUCATIONAL SERVICES

Published in 2019 by Britannica Educational Publishing (a trademark of Encyclopædia Britannica, Inc.) in association with The Rosen Publishing Group, Inc.
29 East 21st Street, New York, NY 10010

Copyright © 2019 The Rosen Publishing Group, Inc. and Encyclopædia Britannica, Inc. Encyclopædia Britannica, Britannica, and the Thistle logo are registered trademarks of Encyclopædia Britannica, Inc. All rights reserved.

Distributed exclusively by Rosen Publishing.
To see additional Britannica Educational Publishing titles, go to rosenpublishing.com.

First Edition

Britannica Educational Publishing
J.E. Luebering: Executive Director, Core Editorial
Mary Rose McCudden: Editor, Britannica Student Encyclopedia

Rosen Publishing
Amelie von Zumbusch: Editor
Matt Cauli: Series Designer
Tahara Anderson: Book Layout
Cindy Reiman: Photography Manager
Sherri Jackson: Photo Researcher

Library of Congress Cataloging-in-Publication Data

Names: Niver, Heather Moore, author.
Title: What are temperate deciduous forests? / Heather Moore Niver.
Description: First edition. | New York : Britannica Educational Publishing, in Association with Rosen Educational Services, 2019. | Series: Let's find out! Biomes | Audience: Grades 1–5. | Includes bibliographical references and index.
Identifiers: LCCN 2018010001 | ISBN 9781508106944 (library bound) | ISBN 9781508107088 (paperback) | ISBN 9781508107309 (6 pack)
Subjects: LCSH: Forest ecology – Juvenile literature.
Classification: LCC QH541.5.F6 N58 2019 | DDC 577.3 – dc23
LC record available at https://lccn.loc.gov/2018010001

Manufactured in the United States of America

Photo credits: Cover, interior pages background Vovan/Shutterstock.com; p. 4 DEA/C. Sappa/De Agostini/Getty Images; p. 5 © Encyclopædia Britannica, Inc.; p. 6 Andrii Varvaryuk/Shutterstock.com; p. 7 Charriau Pierre/Photographer's Choice/Getty Images; p. 8 Matt Gibson/Shutterstock.com; p. 9 Aleksander Bolbot/Shutterstock.com; p. 10 Carole Castelli/Shutterstock.com; p. 11 Sam Chrysanthou/All Canada Photos/Getty Images; p. 12 Dugdax/Shutterstock.com; p. 13 Chase Clausen/Shutterstock.com; p. 14 Radius Images/Getty Images; p. 15 © Alan Watson/Forest Light; p. 16 Reimar Gaertner/UIG/Getty Images; p. 17 Konrad Wothe/Minden Pictures/Getty Images; p. 18 Moelyn Photos/Moment/Getty Images; p. 19 Don Johnston MA/Alamy Stock Photo; p. 20 Wayne Lynch/All Canada Photos/Getty Images; p. 21 Cornelius Paas/imageBROKER/Getty Images; p. 22 Liz Weber/Shutterstock.com; p. 23 Chros Moody/Shutterstock.com; p. 24 Anne Ackermann/The Image Bank/Getty Images; p. 25 xPACIFICA/The Images Bank/Getty Images; p. 26 Herman Wong HM/Shutterstock.com; p. 27 Jeff Greenberg/Universal Images Group/Getty Images; p. 28 Karen Kasmauski/National Geographic Image Collection/Getty Images; p. 29 Buyenlarge/Archive Photos/Getty Images.

Contents

Fantastic Forests	4
A Temperate Climate	6
Four Seasons	8
The Forest and Its Trees	10
Other Forest Plants	14
Who Lives in These Woods?	16
Hibernation and Migration	20
Forest Food Chains	22
Food, Fuel, and More	24
Humans and the Forests	26
Conservation Concerns	28
Glossary	30
For More Information	31
Index	32

Fantastic Forests

Forests are fascinating! A large area filled with many trees is called a forest. It is hard to imagine a resource that provides more benefits for humans than do forests. Food, shelter, tools, and fuels are all products of this natural treasury.

Forests grow in almost every part of the world. Every forest is a complex living system made up of thickly growing trees, bushes, vines, and other plants.

There are several different types of forest **biome**. They include the taiga and tropical rainforests.

Another type of forest biome is one in which temperate deciduous

This forest's leaves drop in the fall.

VOCABULARY

A **biome** is a large region of Earth that has a certain climate and certain types of living things.

trees are the native trees. Such forests are found mainly in the Northern Hemisphere. They have four distinct seasons. The trees in a temperate deciduous forest shed their leaves in the fall. A wide variety of plants, trees, and animals grow and live here.

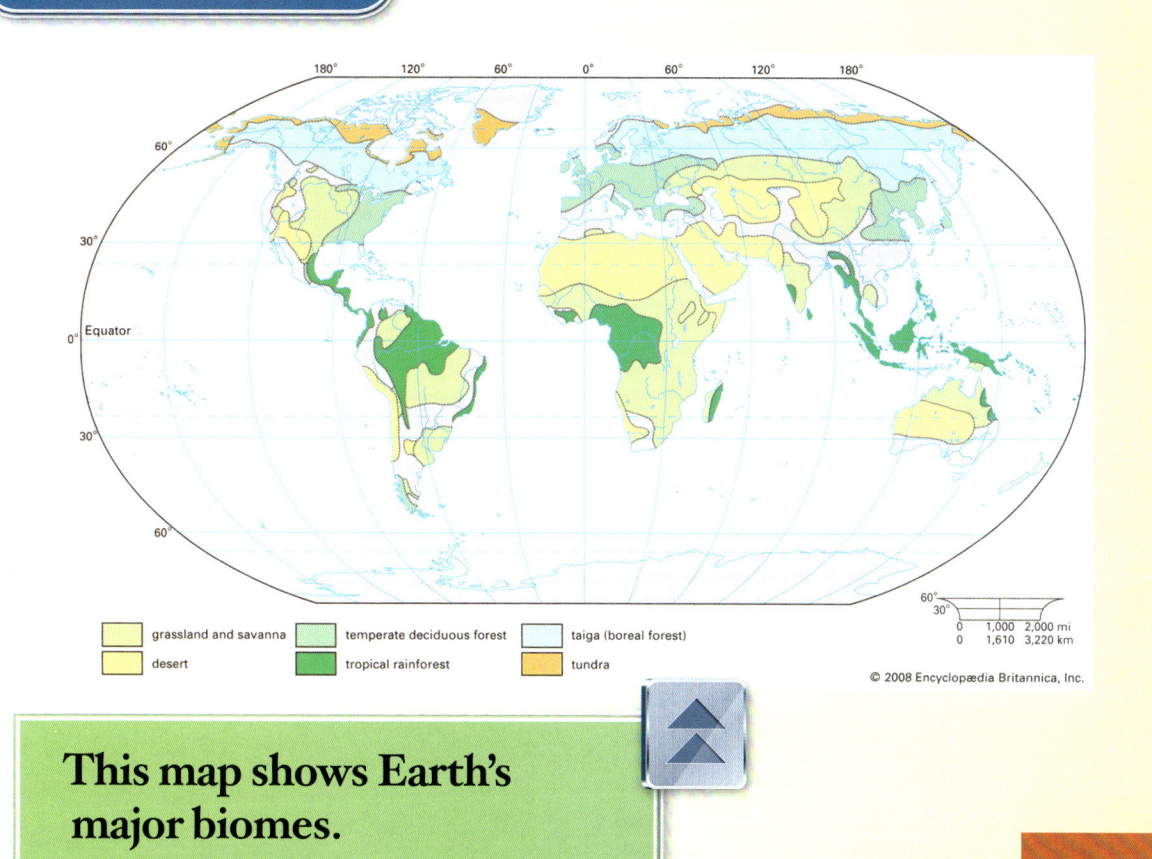

- grassland and savanna
- desert
- temperate deciduous forest
- tropical rainforest
- taiga (boreal forest)
- tundra

© 2008 Encyclopædia Britannica, Inc.

This map shows Earth's major biomes.

5

A Temperate Climate

A temperate climate is mild, which means the temperatures are neither extremely hot nor extremely cold. Temperate deciduous forests have moist, warm summers. They also have cold, frosty winters. They are found in eastern North America, eastern Asia, and much of Europe. These forests are some of the oldest in the whole world.

Winter in a temperate deciduous forest means cold temperatures, ice, and snow.

THINK ABOUT IT

Some trees lose their leaves when there is a drought. Why is this an advantage to the tree?

Not all temperate deciduous forests look the same. They can have different temperatures, moistures, and elevations. So the plants and trees that grow in each one may be different.

Temperate deciduous forests make up one of the wettest major biomes. Only the rainforests are wetter. The average yearly precipitation in a deciduous forest is between 30 and 60 inches (75 and 100 centimeters). Precipitation falls as rain or snow depending on the season.

These forests are one of the wettest biomes.

Four Seasons

Temperate deciduous forests have four distinct seasons: winter, spring, summer, and fall. The average temperature is about 50 degrees Fahrenheit (10 degrees Celsius). Summer season temperatures average about 70°F (21°C).

The trees' leaves all change as the seasons change. In the fall there are fewer hours of daylight and the temperature begins to get colder. Deciduous trees stop making the green pigment known as **chlorophyll** in their leaves. Without the chlorophyll, the

Leaves change color when trees stop making chlorophyll.

> **VOCABULARY**
> **Chlorophyll** is a chemical that makes plants green. It helps plants make food from energy in the sunlight.

other colors in the leaves show up. The leaves turn all kinds of bright colors. They may be vibrant red, yellow, and orange. Eventually the leaves die and drop from the trees.

During the winter, temperatures are usually below freezing. Trees become dormant, or inactive, in winter. When the weather warms up in the spring, trees begin to grow new leaves again.

Temperate deciduous forests are very green in the summer.

The Forest and Its Trees

Temperate deciduous forests have many different species, or kinds, of trees. Most of the trees are hardwoods. They have broad, wide leaves that are perfect for catching the sunlight. The trees need sunlight in order to grow. Oaks, beeches, hickories, and maples are common.

The oaks and beeches in this forest in France are hardwoods.

While deciduous forests have mostly hardwoods, the taiga has mainly softwoods.

COMPARE AND CONTRAST

How are hardwoods and softwoods similar? How are they different?

The taiga is a forest biome that can be found in far northern parts of the world. Softwoods have cones and needles rather than fruits and wide leaves. They tend to keep their needles all year long. Mixed forests with both kinds of trees are located in between the taiga

This mixed forest is located in Valley Provincial Park, in Alberta, Canada.

Tall trees like this majestic oak commonly grow in temperate deciduous forests.

and temperate deciduous forests.

Oaks, elms, birches, maples, beeches, and aspens are common in temperate deciduous forests. Chestnut trees were once common in eastern North America. However, they were almost entirely killed off by a disease called chestnut blight in the early 1900s.

Temperate deciduous forest trees grow to be all different shapes and heights. Many trees in this biome grow to be very tall. Their branches and leaves stretch out to create a canopy. This thick umbrella of leaves blocks a lot of the sunlight from the plants and trees below.

Some **evergreen trees** grow in this biome as well. These include hemlock, spruce, and fir trees.

> **VOCABULARY**
>
> **Evergreen trees** have leaves that remain green and functional through more than one growing season. The leaves do not fall off every year.

The mighty maple tree's wide leaves form a canopy high above the forest floor.

Other Forest Plants

Temperate deciduous forests usually have different plant levels. The lowest is on the forest floor. It is made up of small plants and wildflowers. Lichen, moss, and ferns also grow there. Next there are shrubs. Finally, the highest level is made up of trees.

Many species of shrubs, herbs, and mosses grow in the low light that reaches the forest floor. Flowering plants bloom in the spring. They grow in

Ferns grow on the forest floor of Allegheny National Forest, in Pennsylvania.

> **THINK ABOUT IT**
>
> Most plants in a deciduous forest grow well in shade. Why do plants like that thrive in such forests?

the sunlight before the trees grow their new leaves and block the sun. Then their blooms wither, or dry up, until the next spring. One forest can have as many as one hundred species of plants!

Plants adapt to living under the high trees. If tall trees block the light, the shorter plants lean toward the sunlight.

Flowering bluebells cover the floor of a temperate deciduous forest in Scotland.

Who Lives in These Woods?

Many different kinds of animals — mammals, birds, insects, reptiles, and others — call this forest biome home. Forest mammals include squirrels, rabbits, deer, foxes, wolves, bears, and many others. Asian forests are home to some species of monkeys. Many kinds of birds, such as owls, pigeons,

Bears are one of the bigger animals that make their home in this forest biome.

and migrating songbirds, live here, too. Reptiles and amphibians that live in forests include snakes, frogs, salamanders, and turtles.

Animals living in this biome are adapted to live in different parts of the forest. Some live on the ground while others live in the trees. They each have features that help them survive in the different areas. For example, some animals that live in trees are good at climbing.

Compare and Contrast

How is life different for animals that live on forest floors compared to those that live in the trees? How are their conditions similar?

A snail creeps across some moss on a forest floor in Germany.

Many animals, especially the browsers—such as deer and elk—use the temperate deciduous forest for shelter. They spend much of their time along the forest edge. Here they eat grasses and brush. They retreat to the woods for safety. Other animals, such as bears, can find the nuts and smaller animals that they feed on deeper in the woods. They also enjoy the berries and roots they find along the forest edge and in clearings.

Animals that live in these forests have to deal with changing seasons. They have to deal with hot

Deer are common in the forests of eastern North America.

Think About It

Animals living in a deciduous forest are often the same color as the ground. How do you think this helps them survive?

weather in summer. When the leaves fall from the trees, there are fewer places to hide from predators. In winter the temperatures can be very cold, and food is hard to find. Some animals move south or hibernate to deal with the cold.

This fox's thick fur keeps it warm though the chilly winters in its forest home.

Hibernation and Migration

Hibernation is one way that animals deal with the harshness of winter. They curl up in a safe place and stay there until winter ends. Hibernating animals seem almost dead. They barely breathe. Their body temperature is near the freezing mark. In warmer weather they return to their regular activities.

Animals like bears change their activities in the winter but are

Black bears sleep through the cold winter.

not true hibernators. They spend most of the winter asleep, but their body temperature barely drops. A bear will move around if woken up.

> **THINK ABOUT IT**
>
> Birds fly to warmer areas during the winter. Why do you think it benefits birds to migrate?

Some animals simply do not stick around when the weather gets cold. Many mammals, birds, fishes, insects, and other animals move from one place to another at certain times of the year. This movement is called migration. Most animals migrate across water, land, or air. Many birds and bats in northern parts of the world fly south for the winter.

These cranes are migrating over a forest in the fall.

Forest Food Chains

Each living thing in a forest has a role to play—as a producer, a consumer, or a decomposer. Plants are producers. They make their own food through a process that is called **photosynthesis**.

> **Vocabulary**
>
> **Photosynthesis** is the process by which green plants use sunlight to make their own food.

Animals are consumers. They eat, or consume, plants or other animals. Sometimes consumers are

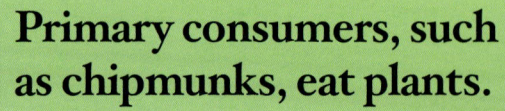

> Primary consumers, such as chipmunks, eat plants.

further divided into primary consumers, secondary consumers, and tertiary consumers. Primary consumers feed on plants. Secondary consumers feed on primary consumers, and tertiary consumers prey on secondary consumers.

Bacteria and other living things that cause decay are decomposers. Decomposers break down the waste products and dead tissue of plants and animals. They return nutrients to the soil, where new plants grow. The way that producers, consumers, and decomposers provide nutrients for one another is called a food chain.

Mushrooms are decomposers. They often grow on fallen trees.

Food, Fuel, and More

Forests are known as the lungs of the planet. They supply a huge amount of Earth's oxygen. The trees of a forest give off oxygen as part of photosynthesis. Animals need the oxygen to breathe. Forest trees also help to protect soil from erosion. They block the forces of wind and water that wear away the land. In addition, forests offer a peaceful place for all kinds of activities. Some people head to the forest for hiking, camping, bird watching, and exploring nature.

This family is hiking in a forest in northern New York.

COMPARE AND CONTRAST

What kinds of things do both people and animals depend on forests for? Which are only necessary for people?

Many natural resources come from the world's forests. Forests provide humans with many things. For example, we get food, wood, fuel, natural fibers, and other materials. These resources may be made into furniture, shelter, paper, medicines, and many other products.

Mushroom hunters must be careful. While some types of mushrooms are safe to eat, others types are poisonous.

25

Humans and the Forests

Humans live in the temperate deciduous forest biome, too. But unfortunately our presence is not always positive. For example, our cars and other activities result in acid rain. Acid rain weakens trees and makes them less healthy. Humans cut down forests to make space for farming or to use the wood for timber. Humans have also introduced invasive plants and animals. These plants and animals can be damaging to the forest. They may create new competition and drive out the native plants and animals.

The emerald ash borer can hurt trees.

THINK ABOUT IT

More humans live in the temperate deciduous forest biome than in any other biome. Why is that? Think about the weather there compared to the weather in other biomes, including the dry deserts and extremely cold taiga.

As a forest ages or changes, it affects all the living things in it. People who work in forestry study the life cycles of trees and other forest plants. They also work to prevent the spread of tree diseases, keep trees safe from harmful insects, and control forest fires.

A ranger *(right)* teaches visitors about a forest.

Conservation Concerns

For thousands of years people have been cutting down the world's temperate deciduous forests. They use the wood and make room for farms and cities. Now many of the world's forests are in danger of disappearing. Deforestation—the cutting down of forests—is a threat not just to the trees but also to all the other animals and plants that make these forests their home.

Luckily, people are working to conserve, or save, the world's forests. Governments create

Many of the trees in this Tennessee forest have been cut down.

national forests, state parks, and wilderness preserves to protect forests. In these places, forests are left in their natural state for people to enjoy. And we want to enjoy our deciduous forest biomes for a very long time.

Think About It

To save natural forests people sometimes plant tree farms. As workers cut down the trees grown on these farms, they plant new trees to replace them. What other ways can humans save forests?

Catoctin Mountain Park preserves land in Maryland.

Glossary

adapt To make or become suitable.

climate The weather found in a certain place over a long period of time.

conservation A careful preservation and protection of something.

decompose To break down through chemical change; rot.

elevation How high a place is above sea level.

erosion The act of wearing away by the action of water, wind, or glacial ice.

forestry The science of caring for forests.

herbs Seed-producing plants that do not develop long-lived woody tissue but die down at the end of a growing season.

invasive Relating to plants and animals that are introduced into an area where they are not native and that tend to spread and disrupt the native plants and animals.

lichen A kind of plantlike living thing made up of algae and a fungus growing together on a solid surface (as a rock or a tree).

migration The movement of animals from one place to another at certain times of year.

moss Any of a class of plants that have no flowers and produce small leafy stems at their tips and that grow in patches like cushions clinging to rocks, bark, or damp ground.

Northern Hemisphere The half of Earth that lies north of the equator.

nutrient A thing that provides nourishment.

pigment A substance that gives color to other materials.

precipitation Water that falls from the sky.

preserve An area where natural resources (as fish, game, or trees) are protected.

tissue Groups of cells in living things that work together to do a job.

For More Information

Books

Boothroyd, Jennifer. *Let's Visit the Deciduous Forest* (Lightning Bolt Books: Biome Explorers). Minneapolis, MN: Lerner Publishing Group, 2017.

Grady, Colin. *The Deciduous Forest Biome.* New York, NY: Enslow Publishing, 2017.

LaPlante, Walter. *There's a Forest in My Backyard!* New York, NY: Gareth Stevens, 2017.

Spilsbury, Louise, and Richard Spilsbury. *Forest Biomes.* New York, NY: Crabtree Publishing, 2018.

Websites

Kids Do Ecology
http://kids.nceas.ucsb.edu/biomes/temperateforest.html

Minnesota Department of Natural Resources
http://www.dnr.state.mn.us/biomes/deciduous.html
Facebook: @MinnesotaDNR; Twitter: @mndnr

NASA's Earth Observatory
https://earthobservatory.nasa.gov/Experiments/Biome/biotemperate.php
Facebook: @nasaearth; Twitter: @NASAEarth

National Parks Service: Eastern Deciduous Forest
https://www.nps.gov/im/ncrn/eastern-deciduous-forest.htm
Facebook and Twitter: @NPSNCRN

Index

acid rain, 26
Asia, 6, 16

bacteria, 23
biome, 4–5, 7, 11–13, 16–17, 26–27, 29

canopy, 13
chlorophyll, 8–9
consumer, 22–23

decomposer, 22–23
deforestation, 28

erosion, 24
Europe, 6
evergreen, 13

forestry, 27
fuel, 4, 24–25

hardwood, 10–11
herb, 14

insect, 16, 21, 27

North America, 6, 12
Northern Hemisphere, 5

oxygen, 24

photosynthesis, 22, 24
pigment, 8
plant, 4–5, 7, 9, 13, 26–27, 28–29
  flowering, 14–15
  food chain, 22–23
precipitation, 7
preserve, 29
producer, 22–23

shelter, 4, 18, 25
softwood, 11
sunlight, 9, 10, 13, 15, 22

taiga, 4, 11–12, 27

temperate deciduous forest
  animal life, 5, 16–19, 20–21, 22–23, 24–25, 26, 28
  climate, 5, 6–7, 8
  conservation, 28–29
  defined, 4–5
  food, 4, 9, 18–19, 22–23, 24–25
  hibernation and migration, 17, 19, 20–21
  human influence, 4, 25, 26–27, 29
  plant growth, 4–5, 7, 9, 14–15, 22–23, 26, 28–29
  seasons, 5, 6–7, 8–9, 13, 18–19, 20–21
  types of trees, 5, 10–13
  temperature, 6–7, 8–9, 19, 20–21
tropical rainforest, 4

3 1333 04780 1830